Behind the Little House

Behind the Little House

William L. Penniman
(1901-1994)

Writers Club Press
San Jose New York Lincoln Shanghai

Behind the Little House

Writers Club Press
an imprint of iUniverse.com, Inc.

For information address:
iUniverse.com, Inc.
5220 S 16th, Ste. 200
Lincoln, NE 68512
www.iuniverse.com

ISBN: 0-595-17364-0

Printed in the United States of America

Contents

Preface

In 1993, after ninety-one years of active living, our father moved into a nursing home. He had lost the ability to care for himself or help his wife with the activities of daily living. Some vestiges of the spirit that carried him through life's adventures remained—his humor delighted the caretakers of his body. His heart and lungs remained strong, though his legs no longer held him upright and his mind no longer held him firmly in reality. His days were spent mostly in dreamy recollection, and there was much to dream about. We hope he was dreaming when he died on December 2, 1994.

He led an unusual childhood as the only son of a country doctor and strong-willed mother who had been a secretary to a state senator. His older sister died tragically in infancy, before his birth. As a youngster (and an only child), he received much attention from his parents. In his teen years, however, he was moved from school to school and, finally, cut loose to fend for himself. While in high school, he lived away from home in a rooming house with some other boys, fixing his own meals on a hot plate. He attended college at the University of Illinois where he graduated in 1924 with a degree in industrial administration.

After college, he lived adventurously. He worked in the hills of California at a construction camp, shipped out on a freighter carrying high-octane fuel through the Panama Canal, and shot running jack rabbits with a Winchester 94 while living in Texas and working as a construction laborer at a resort being built on the Gulf of Mexico. During the depression he married and moved his bride onto a truck farm in Illinois. When his first child was born he joined the shoe manufacturing company he served for over thirty years.

At retirement he moved to a farm that his father had bought and lived on after his retirement. Our father, during his retirement, spent almost twenty-five years conquering erosion, raising soybeans and corn, developing building sites on untillable sections of the land, and pondering the meaning of life. As he pondered, life continued. His wife of thirty-eight years, our mother, died unexpectedly. He mourned her loss, but went on with life—falling in love again with a widow of exceptional spirit. He married her in his seventieth year with his son as best man. For twenty years he and this sparkling lady shared their lives with each other, and with their combined children, grandchildren and great grandchildren.

After his first wife's death, he sold the farm house they (and his parents before them) had lived in, and moved to town. But on a small plot of ground on the farm, he built a getaway house, where he frequently rested and pondered. It is more a shed than a house and quite plain. On the outside back wall, however, away from any casual observer, are painted a strange array of geometric shapes and lines. Always a very private person, he has shared their meaning with only a few of us. We wrote down most of what he said so we would not forget the symbolism he used to express his views of life. There are sections on the meaning of life and its highs and lows. There is passion and sex (not necessarily combined), the water and boats (one of his passions never fully realized), and aspirations compared to realizations. There is profundity to be found behind this little house, but only a few were allowed to know his thoughts and they had to ask.

William L. Penniman

The poems in this book were written by our father over the last seventy years. We found them as we looked through his files for a collection of short stories we knew he had written. When we found these poems we realized they said more about him than we ever could. Most are undated, but some make reference to events we remember, so we can guess at their possible date of origin. Their meaning, however is usually clear—if not always simple. Best of all, this "look behind his little house" does not need explanation. These poems are for all of us to have without asking. Now that he is gone, they mean even more to us.

Sally Eaton

David Penniman

(his editors and loving children)

~ ADVICE TO A DAUGHTER

He will say that stars are in your eyes
That you are the moon in clouded skies
For which he is hopefully reaching
Or the guiding planet he's seeking
He'll probably bring in the Milky Way
Or the Borealis, in a silky way.
You'll hear of life as a shell that is empty.
(He's the nut, is the pun that tempts me,
that's gone from the shell of a life that's
    empty).
He'll live on the moon or in a shell
But his thoughts on planets* chiefly dwell.
Daughter, this I started to tell
The sky has no monopoly
on bodies that are heavenly.

*Webster—a heavenly body

∾ THE AMERICAN SPIRIT

The dictator's heel, the fist of mail
The fear that democracy will fail
Think nothing of it, let it ride
So long as over the country side,
While hoping to build a ten room lodge
Rugged souls will live in a two-car garage.

❧ *AWAKENING*

My ego is just full of baloney
It likes to imply I'm the great one and only
Then a stranger will slap my back
or grasp my hand a bone to crack
With a hello, Jake, or Tom or Phil
Well—it happens my name is Bill
And the stranger is right, the ego away
I'm just another guy

~ *BABY DAVE*

Arms and legs a going
Like a bug upon its back
Eyes gleaming—turning—seeking
Noises, voices, shining lights
Little half moon smile revealing
Not a single touch of white

∿ THE BIG FAMILY

You pile into the day coach
Kind mother, thin father
and seven more
From two to fourteen years
With your three big suitcases
Tied round with ropes,
a paste board box
Held with a strap
Innumerable packages and bundles
and a portable phonograph
With stacks of records
You would!
The fun begins
The phonograph starts
Suzie drops her apple
Mary washes it off
Freddie opens the window
So he can put his head out
Katy wants it closed
Mom—it's too cold
Father goes into the smoker
Mother leans back
Closes her eyes
The fun goes on

❧ *A BOY*

He likes to wear old battered hats
And pants with patchy knees
But a shirt without a collar
Gives him allergies.

He likes to step on peanut shells
And stamp his heel on matches
But a pair of shoes with squeaky soles
Brings up his ire in batches.

❧ *THE CANDLE IS GONE, BUT THE WICK STILL BURNS*

The age of true maturity is at the door
If past mistakes can be repeated, nevermore.

∾ *CAREFUL DRIVER*

When driving the legal speed
What vehicles do I exceed?
One horse shays, Model T's
Sick rabbits, sluggish bees
Those who use their feet to travel
Up hill trucks filled with gravel
I would go so far to say
I couldn't pass the time of day
Those with whom I want to do it
In a burst of speed eschew it

↩ *COED'S DEFENSE*

(written in 1920 while in college)
Men have smoked since 1704
Maybe a flock of decades more
But women began around 1910
So I think it's just mean of men
To snarl "pretender" "hypocrite"
Given time—we'll learn to like it

COW'S HEAD THROUGH THE FENCE

With twist and turn, and crack of her back
And extra shove where wire was slack
The idiot cow horned through to find
Other-side grass of the very same kind.
The clear conclusion made so far?
Stay in the pasture where you are.
An ugly head is reared. And how!
Human creature is not a cow.

∾ *CRAZY BUSINESS*

Quick lunch business is a wet rag always
    wiping.
Gasoline station business is crowding gasoline
    into a tank
always running over.
Mailman business is always magazines and
    circulars with a
dog snapping.
Auto parking lot business is always scratching
    fenders with the
key left in.
Laundry business is always a steamy smell
    with the buttons
pulled off.
        and
            so
                on and on.

THE DAILY ENQUIRER

Dad, what makes a whistle blow?
And where does steam go?
Why does a hill slope down?
What's underneath the ground?
More ground? Dad? Is there?
And why can't I see air?
What makes a fire hot?
A pest? Aw Dad, I'm not!
I just wanna know!
What does make a whistle blow?
All right Dad, I'll be still
But is a valley an upside down hill?
What's littler than a gnat?
And why!?!
Sniff! sniff! Did Dad do that?
What makes him act so?
I just wanna know.

A DREAM—WITH RESERVATIONS

The things I want are really few
A little place with an ocean view
A little boat with bunks for four
Some rugged country to explore
But then of course I want to keep
The things I have—or those I seek
Would be just unimportant toys,
Uncomplemented by present joys.

﹏ *FAMOUS CLEARINGS*

THE LITTLE CLEARING IN THE WOODS

You need a place to build a fire?
The timber line is three miles higher.

You seek a spot to pitch a tent?
If one is near, it's an accident.

This little clearing of fame and fable!
This much is clear. The place is unstable.

THE MAN BEHIND US WITH THE THROAT

Now what, I ask, can be stuck in it.
By sound, I swear, there's a duck in it.

THE AIR THAT IS CLEARED BY A FIGHT

Brawlers declare a brawl clears the air
While spectators choke on blood and hair.

(FASHION NOTE-OLD TIME CORSETS COMING BACK)

Shoes with holes instead of toes
Shoes that wobble, jump, and flop
Hats that lean upon the nose
Hats that perch way up on top
Padding here and padding there
Upswept, downswept, sideswept hair.
Pooh—mere trifles—these.
Fashion now decrees
Corsets with strings
Waspy-waisted things
Busty above and bulgy below
Will I wear one? The answer is NO.
Go on, Dame fashion, make a fuss
Threaten, plead, cajole, even cuss.
Your strongest pressure will not prevail
Untouched I'll be by your loudest wail
For (Gosh, I'm thankful) I'm a male.

☙ *FICKLE HEREDITY*

Back in the branches of my family tree
There is reason to think that I might be
A surgeon keen
A captain of the sea
An entrepreneur
A restauranteur
The leader of a band
A ladies man
A shady character
An exaggerating narrator.
So it's a mystery to me
That I'm not one of these
But in the shuffle of genes
For better or worse
Turned out with a desire
To be a maker of verse

THE FLIRT

Yesterday on the city street
In sweltering midday heat
A garbage truck came creaking by
On the front seat high
Sat Casanova
With wink and leer and raised eyebrow
For pretty girl and shopping frau.
I wonder what it takes in man
To sit upon a garbage van
And try to flirt
Surrounded by romantic smells
Of coffee grounds and grapefruit shells.

∾ *FLORIDA SWAMPS*

Leaning trees hung with moss,
Like be-whiskered old men,
Bending over pools of tears
Waiting for mouldy death
or the subdividers stakes
When tear-pools will disappear—
Become silvery lakelets.
Trees bent and arched
Seem to straighten
and lose their age
Appear stately.
Moss drapes artistically
no longer mournful.
Streets with names,
Watermains and walks
Make swamps a paradise
And greedy men—fools;
Until the bubble breaks;
Then age and tears return
To swamps and men.

~ *FLORIDA TREE*

A tree like a French Poodle's tail!
That tall, spindly trunk
With tip of frazzled branches
High in the air
Huh! Dame Nature
After all, You're a woman,
With your whims.

FOUNTAINS OF GUSH

On and on it flows and flows
A limitless supply
One women with her "she saids"
The other with "tchs!" and "my, my!"

∼ *THE FUTURE*

The glad expectancy of fortune's smile
That gives it's thrill to youth
A battered veteran sees unveiled
As ignorant hope of things unknown.

∾ THE GIRL I'VE NEVER SEEN

Your lips are so pretty
Your hair so smooth and neat
Your eyes a quiet gray
Capable—your firm small body seems
Yet womanly and appealing
With trim ankles and bewitching knees
You seem so genuine and desirable.
Though I wonder if you would be the joy
That imagination makes you

~ GOOD BOSS

He must drive and push and force
And make it seem like leading
Seek faults and flaws and weakness
And make it seem like helping
Castigate or condone—whichever suits the
    purpose
Using privately his safety valve of humor
Keeping his generosity under shackles
His sympathy well hidden
His mind collecting the scatterings of waste
To mold into nuggets of profit

∽ HAS HE NEVER BEEN HUNGRY?

Three men ordered, the room stayed quiet.
Then spoke the fourth for his special diet.
Pompously he said and loud and clear,
Some soup, a bowl, no cup—you hear?
Sandwich, ah—cheese, it Swiss must be
On white bread only—butter sparsely.
A pot of tea, and green, no other.
Details, details, words. Oh, brother.
A stomach could never be this exacting,
His ego he feeds with overacting.

HIGH SCHOOL FLIVER

Fenders flopping in the breeze
Gasket leaks that hiss and sneeze
Scrambled arms and legs and noise
Much of each for seven boys
Much too much of lettered wit
Plastered over all of it

Go on, Lizabeth, play like hell
Though I know, I'll never tell
You were once our joy and pride
My family's Sunday motor ride.

∽ *HIM OF HATE*

He is my favorite blight
This guy of mental might
This personality kid
This human giant squid
Who uses words instead of ink
To cover any personal stink
Or build a vocal monument
On which to place accomplishment.
To some it may be salesmanship
To me it smells like bullmanship.

∽ A HISS FOR THE HERO

The story I'd rather avoid than not
Uses amnesia to rescue the plot.

∾ HOT HIGHWAY VACATION

Hot fish, hot tamales, hot dogs
Hot legs of chicken and frogs
Hot youngsters' sweaty wrath
Hot Mama who wants a bath
Hot Dad who'd gladly trade
For a spot of back-home shade.

∾ *ICE COATED TREES*

Freezing rain builds a cast
From twig to trunk
Bending long limbs pitifully
Until fibers break and tear
Leaving white wounds
For wind and sun to cauterize

INDEFINITE OBJECTION

The character I'd barely miss
Refers to anything as "this".

☙ *INSATIABLE MAN*

College boys and salty sailors
Have eyes alive for this and that
But look around you if you think
A banker, broker, or diplomat
Can't twist his neck 180 degrees
For a pretty pair of wind-blown knees.

∾ *INSPIRATION*

If I were a poet
On my typewriter I'd peck
Writing a sonnet
"To a Woman's Neck"

If I were an artist
Broad canvas I'd bedeck
To create my masterpiece
"Woman with a Neck"

✌ JUNE—ROOM

What is so rare as a day in June?
Hot water in a public wash room.

⟋ *JUS' ADD A PROP*

Old Black Mandy
Liv in a shack
Nex' to Deacon Brown's
Dat shack was old
Like Mandy was
De top of it
Lean right ovah
To'ad de groun
De Deacon worry
Sposin' say he
Dat shack fall
Hit ma house
Kill ma hawg
Bust ma tree.
Mandy, da Deacon say
Yo house do lean
Tain't safe
Fo' yo' o me
So Mandy prop
Dat shack o'hers
An if Deacon worry
Mandy say "Sho"
An jus add a prop
Biam by Mandy die
An do yo know

Dat pile o props
De Deacon use
Fo his wood fah
It las' all wintah
Ain't tat shameful
Make po' ole daid woman
Fetch fah wood
Fo' lazy deacon.

∽ *JUST LOOKING ON*

No, Thank you, sir
I do not swim
I thank you, sir
You keep your rod
The rushing stream
The leaping game
Are life to some,
But only flashes
of life to me

LET'S BYPASS THE PASS

My wife, a bright-eyed little filly,
Tours in a manner extremely silly.
At the wheel, she holds it steady
Follows all rules, all reflexes ready
But give her a map! Lord, Oh love her
There's no restraint, no sky above her.
The straightest route is the way she goes,
No bridges, no gas, no surface. Who knows?
We're not a horse opera, I exhort,
The unkindest cut is the one that's short.

LITTLE BOY—AGE THREE

Our little boy, whose age is three
Surely will a philosopher be
While being busy at his play
This is what I heard him say
"I have a little bit of lots"
Plainly said with happy thoughts,
I was nearer thirty-three
Before the knowledge came to me
That it is not just quantity
Of any one commodity
That brings one's ship up to the docks.

LITTLE DAVE—AGE FOUR

Little Dave aged four
Has friends galore
But there are one or two
He strives to eschew
Recently one got in his hair
and his anger in a flare
Evolved a hex, a lulu an AIXX
The name I should write
on a sheet of tissue
and with a flush
he would close the issue

MAN MEDITATIONS

Young men, in the spring, have fancies.
    All year thru
    Old men do.

Young men have fervor and ardor.
    Old men who vie, or try
    Have occlusions and die.

Young men yell and fiddle and diddle.
    Old men cackle, whittle
    Sittle and spittle.

～ *ME*

I'd rather explore a lonely spot
Than round the city's most brilliant block
A broken wreck on a deserted coast
A town abandoned to a miner's ghost
A rusty ship at a rotting pier
I think I must be rather queer
To pass up the city's gayety and glamour
For some man-forsaken panorama.

∿ *MEOW*

A perfect stranger, I heard her say
And when the subject changed direction
It soon became as plain as day
Why only a stranger could rate perfection.

∽ MODERN WIFE'S PLEA

Oh husband mine, I do implore
Come home to me and our children four
Please break this bond with vises and rakes
Do show you have the strength it takes
To come home from the hardware store

(reprinted with permission of *The Saturday Evening Post*)

～ *MONSTER*

A glistening monster with tail fins high
That glares to the rear with bloodshot eye,
Its greasy belly hugging ground.
Where is this creature to be found?
A swamp a cave, where does it live?
With us! The genus automotive.

⌒ *MOONLIGHT*

White moon floating in a darkened sky
A cold reflector of stolen light
Melting virgin's restraint
Banishing contentment
In old men and lone dogs

❧ MY ERROR

The waiter brought an artichoke
I ordered it, I must confess
But now I'd like to choke the bloke
Oh George, wheelbarrow away this mess.

MYSTERY INGREDIENT

Don't buy it—refrain
Wait! What does it contain?
Toothpaste—gasoline
Gargle— polyethylene
Each must have the mystery hex
K3PU or NTZ2U or just plain X
Here is the station break. Hold!
What of utmost importance must be told?
Hear! It contains ethylpolydane
And listeners must contain—
Themselves.

∿ *A NEGRO BOY*

You laugh—say a word or two
With rolling eyes and glistening teeth;
You dance—with flinging arms
Flashing breath, shuffling feet;
Life seems to be one broad grin.
Then you grow up—
Dig ditches, shovel dung
Work in dank, smelly places;
But still you laugh
Leisurely and loud
Wah—Wah—Wah
And people a block away
Hear and smile.

~ *A NEGRO SHACK*

Some boards on end
Topped by a rickety roof
A dragging door that scrapes
The floor of a leaning porch.
Glassless windows, giving a glimpse
Of a black arm and faded lavendar dress
Bracing one end
Destined to stand after the shack
Has fallen or burned
A stone chimney leans miraculously
A monument unto itself

❧ *NEIGHBORLY INTEREST*

We know you are more pecunious
Your larger salary we can't deny
But still we are curious
How you can pay for the things you buy.

∾ *NIGHT BOAT*

Lights on water
Like star clusters on stilts
Sweeping in wide orbits
While candle flames envy

∾ OBEDIENT HUSBAND

Some men are very hard to reach
It takes a call, a yell, a screech
With momma out the window peering
And poppa in the basement leering.
Now I am not that sort of guy,
Your call recieves my quick reply.
Should no response come prompt and clear
Forget the call, I'm nowhere near.

THE OLD DOCTOR

You are the old family doctor
With a kindly smile
and touch of dandruff on your collar
Your thermometer
Is not always washed in alcohol
Sometimes warm water is good enough
Rubber gloves are not always
On your hands
When your city brother
Would need them
But people come from the county's edge
To your small office
Mothers look anxiously up the dark road
For the lights of your car
As they used to listen
For the smacking of your horse's hoofs
In the mud
With your city brothers
Discovering new germs each week
It is hard to understand
How you make sick people well

~ ONE BIG UNHAPPY FAMILY

It seems to be a truth evident
That 96 and 3/4 per cent
Of all who are subject to stress and strain
Eventually become a trifle neurotic
So why not make us all the same
And burn our literature on psychoses
Designed to alleviate neuroses
Then educate the rugged minority
In tics, repressions and inferiority
It seems the sensible thing to do
If what we hear is true
That all of us in this great nation
Are headed for regimentation

∾ *PET IRK*

I can stand the sweltering afternoon heat
The fire in the pavement coming thru
   to my feet
An undershirt that clings to my hide
Or trickles of perspiration down my side
Even shorts that climb and twist sideways
Aren't as annoying on August days
As an oscillating fan
That blasts papers from my hand
And bothers my hair like crawling flys
It's the things persistence that I despise
As it comes and goes with a sleepy drone
I don't mind the heat if I'm let alone.

A POACHED EGG
ON TOAST

There you sit on your crusty perch
So refined—so genteel!
Squeamish people
With thin, sharp noses
All friends of yours.
But for all your nicety
It takes so little
To make you just
A yellow smear
I'd rather be
A hard boiled egg
That tries at least
To keep its yellow hidden

A crazy thing to say?
A crazier way to say a thing!

❧ PROGRESS

This hunger in man
That neither food nor drink
Learning nor love
Will satisfy
Deep as the soul
Vital as hate
Offering simplicity,
Good or Greed?

THE PROSPECTOR

Your eyes see the rainbow's end
Buried in the distant mountain
You are honest, sincere
Your knotted hands
Do not match
With soft words and smooth ways
Some shake their heads when you talk
Some pause and walk sheepishly to the bank.
Usually you fail
But you have an enduring spirit
Sometimes you win and the winnings slip away
Just as your life slips away
Sliding down the side
of a rainbow that has no end.

PTAxiom

As I drove on a country road
Considerably slower than faster
I saw five mamma cows
munching in a pasture
mammas they were I'm sure
Because they were mature
And to prove I don't reason by halves
Nearby were five frolicking calves.
They pranced and danced with rear end
    motions
Until five mammas got similar notions
And with equal spirit, though far less grace
Mammas cut capers, utterly a disgrace.
Though heavy beneath, these bovine mothers
Romped with the kids like sisters and brothers
If a dumb ox of a cow knows this she should do
Then IQish parents should too.

∿ *THE RIVER*

Smashing, tearing, roaring—wild!
A raging giant out to kill.
Calm, companionable, softly singing
A friend to work-tired men
This moody river.

ROADSIDE SIGNS

Hot tamales, hot dogs
Hot fish, hot legs of frogs
Hot shower bath
Hot this and that
All this heat
In season
Is one reason
Summer travelling
Is frazzling

∽ *RULE FOR RULE MAKING*

Rules abound for living, for loving, for
  repenting
Pressing in, governing, controlling—
  unrelenting.
The following rule for rule makers
  consternation.
In all things moderation, including
  moderation.

SALLY'S FACE

Little rounded rosy cheeks
Framed with blondest "bayds"
Eyes that harbor imps and angels
Lips that leave ingenues heartless
Chubby throat with childish creases
There to capture playtime's grime

∾ *SERENITY*

The temper of a little spring
The balance of a little wheel
The absence of a little dog
Nipping at the heels
The starving of little doubts
That might be giants

∾ *SEXIOUS ADVICE*

To women who yearn to be gooey with
   glamour
To be the type for whom men clamor
To be wanted, desired, and seductive
This suggestion will be productive
Go through busy-street puddles fast
Give arm signals as you always do
Drive a car with a horn that blasts
When light flashes red, sneak on through
And many men that you pass near
Will long to lay hands on you, my dear.

SHORT SAYINGS FROM SADLY PARTING LOVERS ADAPTED TO EVERYDAY LIVING

Go, please go, and don't look back
Postman, our dog is on your track.

Don't move, dear one, stay just as you are
Living cost index, you're now up too far.

'Til your return I hang suspended
Hurry, hurry, stepladder's upended.

SONNET OF MOTHERHOOD

White and soft and fluffy
Blowing on the line
Cold and wet and soppy
In very little time

SUMMER
AFTERNOON
IN THE SLUMS

A cushion on the window sill,
Two elbows resting on it
To 'frame' a face between cupped hands
A pair of eyes with languid gaze
That lazily search the street below.
For what, only God would know.

SUMMER DRIVE

It is not the noise
That disturbs my poise
Nor the spots and splashes
That come like flashes
But I can't see why
Bugs that can fly
In any direction
Must make a selection
of a windshield clean
For hari kari's obscene

⤳ *SUMMER NAUSEA*

The leeward side of a packing plant
The low-tide effluvia of a tidal flat
The heaviest fog from the fruit of a hen
The heady aroma of sty or pen
All these are sweeter—ah sweeter by far
Than the lung-stabbing reek of a soggy cigar

SUMMER SUNDOWN

Through the trees leafy shutters
The shady radiance of the sun
Burns with final warmth
Striving to keep its hot grasp
Alive in the last consciousness
Of a day about to die.

∾ *SUMMER VISITOR*

A full two months' too long to stay
Without a single bit of pay
When you began your yearly visits
We furnished medicine and gadgets
But now we just put up with you
Feel resentful and go kerchoo
And look with hope for killing freezes
You pest, you blight, you those and theses
You old ragweed, you glutton for sneezes

∾ *THE THINKERS*

It was in a book, or I heard it said
I've forgotten where, but it's something I read
It may have come from an eminent thinker
It might have been said by a well-read tinker
But when I'm talking about it to you
I'll probably say before I'm through-
"I've turned this problem all about
And this is the way I've thought it out."
It may be I think that is really true.
When you say the same to me, do you?

TO A LITTLE BOY EATING SALTED PEANUTS

You sit behind me in the movie
and wiggle on the edge of your seat
While you eat salted peanuts
Near my ear
I think there is nothing
So appealing—so hunger-provoking
So all-powered good-smelling
As the aroma of salted peanuts
If you weren't such a small boy
I'd turn right around
Snatch that bag from your hand
and make myself sick
Eating your salted peanuts.

TO PUT IT CRUD-ELY

Oh sing a song. Serenade life,
But write in a descant, a fife
To show awareness (and a forgiving)
For the inevitable crud that comes with living.

✏ *TREES IN THE FALL*

Blankets of color over the hills
Splashes of yellow
Green and brown and red
Blended by distance
To an artists despair

A TROT DOWN THE WELL KNOWN GAMUT

AGONY

Of such degree, in reality, can never be
The equal of a choir director's facial frenzy.

LOVE

No panting passions live as do
The sticky gifts from a little issue.

FRUSTRATION

One element on which it thrives;
Polite control of human drives.

NAUSEA

Indubitably, there is much of it
Although we try to act above it.

ACHING

Although not rated as basic, truly
From back to aft it rules us, unduly.

UNDER AN OLD CLOUD

"New Management" your sign proclaims
Though veiled, the former this defames.
OK, OK. Your point is bearable
Just answer this, is the food still terrible.

∾ *WEAK SISTER*

His will is pivoted,
Swinging with each new doubt.
Always pointing with the wind.
The wind of uncertainty
That comes from all directions.

WHEN WRITING A SPEECH

Eminent authorities all agree
This, the first requisite to be.
Before you begin it
Know what is in it.

∽ WHY?

It really never fails.
The movie shows a feast
of baked fowls with plumed tails
Barbecued boars, and least
But not last, a big roast
When I am on a diet
Of buttermilk and toast.

∾ *THE WINNAH*

Clinch, fair lady, it's time for the bell
Shoe stylists haven't treated you well
Though still on your feet, you're out
At the toe, your heels flop about.
Gone are your shanks, there's none.
It's what upper cuts have done.
But there's nothing left for stylists to do
Except give up—and make you a shoe.

∾ *UNTITLED*

Don't be so cross my wife accused
to be convincing, I excused
If I am gentle you will cry
Indignant, she said No! Just try
It was a pleasure, and I tried
What do you think? She promptly cried.

∾ *UNTITLED*

The light was dim as we drove through.
That cow, I said, looks wide as two
My wife—a bright eyed little filly
Laughed in a manner extremely silly
Why not? she said, ha, ha—because
It is. The woman gave me pause
Maybe dim trouble seems like two
Brace yourself. It might be true

∽ *UNTITLED*

Too far to see, too close to touch
This one big aim I can't quite clutch
If it would come under rein
Reward hereafter I'd disdain
To live with a purpose, with whoops and
    hollers
and not be surprised to have some followers

Editors' note: These last five poems were written by our father while he was in a nursing home. They were very difficult to read and some words had to be imagined to complete the works. His sorrow and his humor were clear, however.

CLASH— WIRE WHEELS

Long white peaceful halls
Change to minor clashes and accidents
As aged speedsters (usually males) accelerate
Lock wire wheels, touch and let out whoops
Quickly subdued by watchful aides about

FALL SNOW

Big flakes, small stuff playing games
With gusty winds, now strong
Now tickly comes down…
Now resting to move

~ *UNTITLED*

There is no age limit who knows
Shapely below the thigh
The skirt almost as high

There is no age limit who knows
Shapely below the knees
Skirt goes above with ease

❧ *UNTITLED*

Halls—corridors—wings—doors
Doors, doors, some with other doors
Don't close big hall door
Some sick, some confused
Some not.
Some get better, damit

∾ *UNTITLED*

Long halls to infinity
Held up by doors
Entrances to caves
Where creatures live

To dwell in minds
Of hall users
With yells and calls
And pleas for help